Fiddler Crabs as Pets
A Fiddler Crab Care Guide

Fiddler Crabs Overview, Sub – Species, Feeding, Husbandry Tips, Distribution, Life Cycle, How to Acquire, Breeding and Ritual Process, Environmental Conservation and Much More!

By Lolly Brown

Copyrights and Trademarks

All rights reserved. No part of this book may be reproduced or transformed in any form or by any means, graphic, electronic, or mechanical, including photocopying, recording, taping, or by any information storage retrieval system, without the written permission of the author.

This publication is Copyright ©2019 NRB Publishing, an imprint. Nevada. All products, graphics, publications, software and services mentioned and recommended in this publication are protected by trademarks. In such instance, all trademarks & copyright belong to the respective owners. For information consult www.NRBpublishing.com

Disclaimer and Legal Notice

This product is not legal, medical, or accounting advice and should not be interpreted in that manner. You need to do your own due-diligence to determine if the content of this product is right for you. While every attempt has been made to verify the information shared in this publication, neither the author, neither publisher, nor the affiliates assume any responsibility for errors, omissions or contrary interpretation of the subject matter herein. Any perceived slights to any specific person(s) or organization(s) are purely unintentional.

We have no control over the nature, content and availability of the web sites listed in this book. The inclusion of any web site links does not necessarily imply a recommendation or endorse the views expressed within them. We take no responsibility for, and will not be liable for, the websites being temporarily unavailable or being removed from the internet.

The accuracy and completeness of information provided herein and opinions stated herein are not guaranteed or warranted to produce any particular results, and the advice and strategies, contained herein may not be suitable for every individual. Neither the author nor the publisher shall be liable for any loss incurred as a consequence of the use and application, directly or indirectly, of any information presented in this work. This publication is designed to provide information in regard to the subject matter covered.

Neither the author nor the publisher assume any responsibility for any errors or omissions, nor do they represent or warrant that the ideas, information, actions, plans, suggestions contained in this book is in all cases accurate. It is the reader's responsibility to find advice before putting anything written in this book into practice. The information in this book is not intended to serve as legal, medical, or accounting advice.

Foreword

Crabs, there are all sorts and all kinds of these wondrous decapods, big and small, that populate and repopulate in and around the world. It is possible that we, everyday people, only know of a fraction of them and are unaware of many of the other sorts. Crabs are pretty popular in historical and pop culture, all you need to do is look around and you will notice them present amongst us in various renditions. These little critters are even depicted in the zodiac and a whole constellation has been named to commemorate these 10-legged critters that need both the water and land to thrive.

You may be surprised how much of a following these little guys have and how entertaining it can be to raise them. Prepping their terrarium will be a joy of a project as you will be able to be creative about the spaces they inhabit. Make sure that you read up on how to best set up a terrarium that will give them the best chance of living a good life comfortably. You can even incorporate other aquatic creatures that also thrive in brackish water like guppies, mollies, ghost shrimp, swordtails and platies.

Today, we zero in on one of the more diverse of crab sorts and we'll learn all about the Fiddler Crab and how to raise them successfully. These tiny little guys are a tad unusual from the regular ones that you would point out for your meal on a menu. These little guys are a bit different (all of them are) from the more common ones we see regularly because of their one massive pincer, which much like other crabs, are purposed for specific uses from courting and mating, to self-sustenance.

The Fiddler Crabs is classified as one of the almost one hundred kinds of crabs from the *Uca* family, and our aim with this book is to impart knowledge on how to raise them as pets in your home. We shall discuss the fascinating rejuvenating process of the fiddler crab during its growth cycle. Get to know the fiddler crab better and discover its unique abilities and talents. You will be tickled to know that these little crawlers are in fact an entertaining bunch that will be great to share space with you in your home.

Whether you came upon this book by chance, or if you are looking to get more information about fiddler crabs specifically, our target is to reveal more about how to acquire and where to acquire these sometimes colorful little fellas. We'll let you in on how to raise them well, provide for their sustenance and to identify medical issues that may come up along the way.

You will learn what it would take for you, and what is expected of you, to care for one and what it would need in terms of habitat, companionship and food. You will also learn about its life span, how big they grow and how many you can comfortably keep and raise. There is a lot more we will be discussing as we go along in order to get you ready for your own little fiddler crab farm. So without further delay, let's get on with the introductions of the fiddler crab and get to know more about these creatures which are important to the balance of ecology.

Table of Contents

Chapter One: Understanding Fiddler Crabs...................... 9

    Male vs. Female Fiddler Crabs................................... 18

    Fiddler Crab's Habitat and Interaction........................ 19

    The Fiddler, The Female, and The Morse..................... 22

Chapter Three: The Life Cycle of a Fiddler 27

    Limb Regeneration... 31

    Molting 34

Chapter Four: Common Modern Day Stressors 37

    Courtship Rituals and Mating Process of Fiddler Crabs.. 39

    Breeding Process of Fiddler Crabs 42

    Co - Dependency of Fiddler Crabs 44

Chapter Five: To Catch or to Buy?.................................. 49

    Where to Buy or Find Fiddler Crabs 51

    How to Catch Fiddler Crabs....................................... 54

Chapter Six: Habitat and Maintenance for Fiddler Crabs.... 59

    How to Set Up Your Fiddler Crab Tank 60

    Feeding Your Captive Fiddler Crabs 69

        Some tips for feeding and husbandry of Fiddler Crabs 70

Chapter Seven: Common Sub – Species of Fiddler Crabs.... 73

    Sub – Species of Fiddler Crabs 75

        Mud Fiddler Crab (*Uca Pugnax*) 75

Sand Fiddler Crabs (*Uca pugilator*) 78

Red-jointed Fiddler Crabs (*Uca Minax*) 80

Chapter Eight: Distribution and Ecology Status 83

Distribution 84

Environmental Status 85

Chapter Nine: Challenges of the Species 89

Accomplishments in Conservation 95

Chapter Ten: Summary and Care Sheet 97

Tips in Taking Care of Fiddler Crabs 104

The Crab in Pop Culture 105

Photo Credits 109

References 111

Chapter One: Understanding Fiddler Crabs

Fiddler crabs are the perfect additions to a terrarium/aquarium that house other crustaceans, like hermit crabs, and fish. With over 90 species of fiddler crabs there will be quite a bit of crabs you can choose from that would be willing to share an environment with other cared for pets in a terrarium. Like most crabs, fiddler crabs shed its shed their exteriors and grow new shells at about 8 weeks interval until they reach full maturity in 2 years.

Chapter One: Understanding Fiddler Crabs

Another thing worth of interest is how fiddler crabs regenerate limbs should they lose a leg or a claw during their growth cycle. Should a male fiddler lose its massive claw, it will regenerate a new claw on the opposite side of the limb that was lost when it molts next.

The fiddler crab is pretty vulnerable once molting is underway and this is due to the soft shells that initially develop at this time. The shell of a crab is basically its protective covering from predators therefore fiddler crabs, like other crabs that molt and rejuvenate their exoskeleton, remain reclusive until such time when the shell is hard and ready. These crabs thrive best in brackish waters and are typically found in areas that have these ecosystems. Fiddler crabs will not be able to thrive in freshwater, therefore it is imperative for the new fiddler crab owner to recognize this important need of the crabs which they need to survive.

There is a vast diversity of fiddler crabs. In fact there are over 90 kinds and subspecies of the *Uca* genus which the fiddler crab is classified under. Fiddler crabs are commonly

Chapter One: Understanding Fiddler Crabs

found in the wild on coastal and seaside beaches, and in the intertidal zones of the coastline. Fiddler crabs along the shores forage for food along the coast.

As the tide recedes, it spends time looking for food that is staple to their diet. When done feeding, the fiddler crab retreats into holes they burrow from the mixture of sand and water. The fiddler crabs sought after by crab pet owners are typically found in areas where salinated muddy bogs are present.

Male and female fiddler crabs are easy to spot and distinguish from each other mainly because the male fiddler crab has one pincer that is bigger than the other. The female fiddler crab on the other hand has smaller claw pincers as compared to its male counterpart. They are semi-terrestrial, brackish crabs that need both land and water to be able to thrive to its fullest.

The fiddler crab is a tiny, 10-legged, sideways-crawling little crab that can reach a mature size of 2 inches

Chapter One: Understanding Fiddler Crabs

across the carapace. The larger claw of the male fiddler crab is used in a number of ways. Not only does the male fiddler crab use its one big claw to defend itself and its territory, the male fiddler crab also uses its one massive claw to court female fiddler crabs. On the other hand, the smaller claw of the male is utilized to sustain itself. It uses its claw to forage for food. The male fiddler also uses its smaller claw as an implement to feed itself.

Speaking of feeding, these little guys are typical scavengers that forage for microscopic grub in the forms of dead plant matter and other aquatic plants like algae and seaweed. The diet of the fiddler crab comes from dead organic matter that can be found along the muddy waters of marsh banks and streams where they can be found. Fiddlers also occasionally feed on dead animals.

You would think that having that massive claw, allows males for bigger feedings, but no. The big claw of the male is used for other purposes, which we will discuss a little further later, and using it as an eating implement is just

Chapter One: Understanding Fiddler Crabs

not one of those. On the other hand, the female fiddler crab uses both of its claws to feed itself.

Most crabs molt and so this goes for the fiddler crab. It is not unusual for the fiddler crab to feed on its shed shell whilst it is in molting and this is fine. In fact it is encouraged, by nature, in order for the crab to get much needed calcium in order for it to grow a strong and sturdy outer layer of protection.

These crabs with their distinct asymmetric claws can usually be found in salt marshes and mangroves, actively foraging for food and spending time on socializing, feeding, courtship and settling disputes. They can also be spotted in muddy and sandy coastlines and beaches of the Western Atlantic and the West coast of Africa.

These little side-scramblers also inhibit the coastlines of the Eastern Pacific and Indo-Pacific waters. Fiddler crabs share the same square-shaped bodies, but unlike other crabs that are difficult to identify by gender, fiddler crabs are

Chapter One: Understanding Fiddler Crabs

easier to tell apart with the male fiddler sporting a massive claw.

An interesting aspect of the male fiddler crab is its ability to regenerate its big claw in the event of it being damaged or cut off, say during a battle for territory. The male fiddler, when it experiences a disconnection of this limb, will actually grow it back on the other arm.

The fiddler crab has become an entertaining addition to many aquariums. The fiddler crab is able to share space with some aquatic creatures like guppies, mollies and ghost shrimps. These small scavengers are fascinating additions to any aquarium because of their active lifestyle of foraging and socializing. They are also pretty entertaining on their own.

Whether you choose to keep only fiddler crabs or if you would much rather have a colorful community of mixed species, you will surely be setting up a tank that will be lively and interactive bunch of creatures that will bring calming joy to you and all those who set eyes upon it. They are not finicky eaters, but they will need to be provided with

Chapter One: Understanding Fiddler Crabs

the proper nutrients they need in order to grow, molt and thrive in their captive condition.

Setting up a tank that will resemble their natural habitat will allow them to live long lives as long as they do not have a predator in their tank and they get the proper nourishment and sustenance. You will also have to consider the water quality you will be using for the tank. Since these little guys thrive on semi-salty water, they will need the same condition of water in their tank. Anything too high or too low will be detrimental to the health and wellness of the fiddler.

These crustaceans are pretty hardy and resilient little crawlers but as long as they have adequate and proper food supply and considering the environmental conditions of the tank, making sure that the temperature, brackish water level and cleanliness of the tank is in check, you will be good to go.

You might be surprised to hear this, but fiddler crabs are also a fine delicacy in some countries. There may not be much meat in them, but they are tasty little things that are not only hunted down by small mammals and birds, they

Chapter One: Understanding Fiddler Crabs

are also quite sought after by humans, but it isn't what we are here for today.

What we will be discussing instead is how to capture or purchase fiddler crabs and most especially, we shall be discussing the needs of the fiddler crab when under your care. We shall be helping you set up a tank that will provide for them the best possible environment that will allow them to live and thrive to their fullest form.

You will find these amusing guys to be a joy to live with their silly looking antics. These groups of crabs are indeed a hardworking bunch with a lot of social skills they use in their everyday lives.

Chapter Two: The Fiddler Crab in Focus

These odd looking creatures of the sea and land, with their strange looking eyes set on stems on the tops of their carapace, are often sought after for their soft, succulent meat or are used as bait. Their hard exoskeleton, covering the insides of the sea critter, acts as a defense against predators of all sorts. It is hunted for food by large aquatic and land-based animals, not to mention humans love them as well. But crabs are not merely sought out for food, they are also excellent pets!

Chapter Two: The Fiddler Crab in Focus

Male vs. Female Fiddler Crabs

Female fiddler crabs are easily distinguished from its male counterparts because it possesses normal looking pinchers that are of the same size. In comparison, the male fiddler crab has one pincer that is ridiculously big for its tiny, compact size which it uses as a defense mechanism to avoid becoming another animal's dinner. And they are some staple favorites of bigger predators that share their ecosystem, whether land-based or air-borne, animals like raccoons and birds like herons and egrets find fiddler crabs to be tasty morsels.

Male fiddler crabs are much more colorful than their female counterparts, sporting colors of purple grey and sometimes blue carapace. They also have distinct brown or black markings on them. These little critters measure up to an inch long and grow to a maximum length of up to 2 inches upon maturity. The major claw of the male can reach up to 2 inches long at the most. The colors of the female fiddler crab is much more subdued than that of the male and their claws are of equal size with no notable enlarged claw like that on the male fiddler.

Not only are their huge pincers used to defend themselves from predators as such, they also use their claws to fight amongst themselves. As much as fiddler crabs travel in packs, they still are pretty territorial creatures that vie for their place in their natural habitat. The male fiddler also uses its large claw to entice and attract a female, initiating visual contact by waving at the female.

Fiddler Crab's Habitat and Interaction

These crabs live in colonial groups and like to travel together, and perhaps another way of nature's way of providing a measure of protection by sheer numbers. These crabs live together in large clusters and can often be sighted fighting for territory, as males fight for the ownership of the slanting burrows they dig out for themselves.

Chapter Two: The Fiddler Crab in Focus

Despite the exertion of male dominance on territorial disputes, fiddler crabs still naturally get from one feeding place to another in large crab clusters. When feeding is on the order of the day, the sight of fiddler crabs going out to dine can be an awesome sight to witness. Fiddler crabs feed on decaying plants that are plentiful on marsh banks, as well as underneath mud and sediment. They also dine on algae that can be found around bogs, streams and lagoons. So goes, for those fiddler crabs that dwell along beach coastlines.

Fiddler crabs burrow about 3 and a half feet deep of slanted tunnels where they hideaway to when not foraging or socializing with other crabs. Fiddler crabs that can be found along marshlands and damp grounds use their walking legs to tunnel their way beneath the damp earth. They play an important role in the ecology of salt-marsh lands since it is due to the feeding and tunneling of the fiddler crabs that the aerate the floor of the marsh.

Chapter Two: The Fiddler Crab in Focus

It has been noted that human intervention and destruction of the natural habitat of the fiddler damage the equilibrium of salt water marsh lands. These little side crawlers are able to thrive in damp ground for extended period because they possess a primitive lung that allows them to breath above ground. However, they are also adapted to live part time underwater. They are able to do this by way of breathing through their gills. Fiddler crabs share the same square shaped physique with a smooth carapace. Their eyes are set atop two movable stems that stick out of the center of their carapace.

These little crabs, named after a fiddle or violin because of their one large claw, are usually found around parts where there is water nearby. They can be found along coastlines, hiding between rocks and burrowing on the beaches, and feed on algae that can be plentiful in these areas. They can also be found in low-salinity waters of bodies like streams and lagoons as well as marsh and bog lands.

Chapter Two: The Fiddler Crab in Focus

Fiddler crabs that are found along swamplands share the area with marsh crabs that are usually herbivores, which may sometimes prey on the fiddlers. Apart from marsh crabs, there are other animals, like birds that prey upon the small fiddler crab. Herons, egrets, swallows and seagulls are some of the more opportunistic predators of these little semi-aquatic, semi-terrestrial critters. Fiddlers are seen in their natural habitat all year round with a short respite of hibernation when they burrow and go underground during the winter months of the year. These crabs also take the opportunity to regenerate their shells underground where they are kept removed from any sort of danger from prey.

The Fiddler, The Female, and The Morse

The fiddler crab is not as uncommon as many would think. They just need to know where to look and these little guys can be found in most places where they inhabit. They are curious little guys who are spritely and always on the move. These little crabs are constantly in action. If they aren't looking for food and feeding themselves, they are busy

Chapter Two: The Fiddler Crab in Focus

tunneling away to make preparations for a suitable place to woo and mate with a female they fancy. Once a rightful burrow is achieved, the male who had just toiled away at it, stands by the mouth of the burrow in the hopes of attracting the attention of a female fiddler crab. How they do this is an amazing thing. The male fiddler crabs produce pulses and vibrations which get the attention of the female fiddler. These pulsation and vibrations, discovered by Japanese researchers, are pretty informative since it delivers a Morse-type signal that gives indication of the stamina and the size of their potential beau.

When mating season begins, and it is time to get it on, some fiddler crab male species build a semi-dome like structure, a mound that is raised, very close to their burrow. Here, they stay near the burrow, as if guarding it. They would then raise their one massive claw and wave at the passing females to get them to come closer to them and their burrow.

Chapter Two: The Fiddler Crab in Focus

Notably, the male fiddler who can raise their claw and wave the longest gets the most success; once the female's attention has been captured by the waving male fiddler, the female approaches closer. The male fiddler would then pursue her further by way of emitting vibrations that would entice her to come even closer, with the intention of getting her into the burrow that the male had built so that they can begin mating.

The discovery made by Japanese researchers about the vibrations and pulsations the males emit to attract females are pretty astounding. They learnt that the acoustic signals are made up of pulses on loop. When the dominant frequency of the pulsations is lower, it would give indication to the females that the male's carapace would be an acceptably large one.

Researchers discovered that when more vibrations was produced the length of the pulses slightly decreased. When the male produces more pulses, the interval between the pulses also increased. It is deduced that the vibrations the males make during courtship sends off signals and indications about the size, stamina and body built of the male to the female fiddler crab. The wave of the huge claw in the air to catch the attention of the female and the production of vibrations go hand in hand in the mating call and dance of the fiddler crabs. These are done in order for the male fiddler crabs to convey their stamina and endurance to the female fiddler crabs.

Researchers also observed the mating of the fiddler crabs. They were curious to find out what happened once the female fiddler crab has been lured into the burrow entrance by their male counterparts. They discovered that the female fiddler crab was more likely to be enticed into entering the male's burrow if they could produce a succession of high rate pulses. Indicating that the female would take their cue from the vibrational signals the males made and decides whether or not they should enter the burrow.

Chapter Two: The Fiddler Crab in Focus

Once inside the burrow, the pulsations and vibrations no longer became a factor for the female and at this point what is important is that the sound structure of the burrow is acceptable to the female in order for them to have a safe haven where they can release larvae.

Chapter Three: The Life Cycle of a Fiddler

The Fiddler Crab is a little creature that is found along swamps, bogs and marshlands. At least these are the areas where fiddler crabs sold in pet stores come from. Fiddler crabs are also found along coastlines of beaches. As of 2007, the count of fiddler crab specie and sub-specie has been tallied up to a whopping 97 recognized sorts. It is known to have a life span of 2 years in the wild and can thrive up to about 3 years in captivity.

Chapter Three: The Life Cycle of a Fiddler

There have even been reports of fiddler caregivers of their fiddler living up to a ripe age of 7 years old and still thriving. So the lifespan of this little guy is all a matter of how the fiddler crab is taken care of to live to its utmost.

A largely diurnal specie, these little crabs are seen to be busiest during daylight and even more active during low tide, when they are able to forage for the sustenance they so need to thrive healthily. They are an active group of crabs that live amongst themselves but have independent burrows. These groups of crabs are constantly working at something, whether it be feeding, cleaning up, fighting for territory, waving at each other (most especially females), fighting off each other and getting burrows ready. They occur in large numbers and are usually seen together foraging for food.

The breeding season for fiddler crabs happens each month. The female spends two week of incubation and another two weeks feeding itself. Mature male fiddler crabs are constantly ready for mating action, and so it is really a

Chapter Three: The Life Cycle of a Fiddler

competition of sorts when the males attempt to woo female fiddler crabs.

It is typical to witness male fiddler crabs fighting over territory as well as the attention and affections of a female. Although it is unusual to see males and females fight, it can sometimes happen. Females of most species have displayed inherent preferences for the mate they choose. In the wild, the mating process and mate selection of the female fiddler crab is a complex one. It is easier to pair off a male and a female fiddler crab under controlled conditions. Not so much in their natural habitat, though.

There are a number of hindrances which may prevent the female from expressing their choice on the male they mate with. Some are constrained, leaving them little choice on who to mate with. Other times, the risk of being eaten by a predator restricts them from venturing out of their own burrows in search of a suitable male candidate. There are also many cases of females refusing the male due to the substandard build of burrows.

Chapter Three: The Life Cycle of a Fiddler

Keep in mind that, burrows are where females stay to incubate their eggs before releasing their eggs to the deep blue, so it is important that the female feels and sees the sturdy construction of a place where they can incubate their eggs in peace away from predators and danger.

Once the female is fertilized, the fiddler crab can be laden with hundreds, even thousands, of eggs that sit in the abdomen of the crab. At this stage, the female fiddler crab is given the nickname sponge crab. Once the eggs are ready to hatch, the female fiddler enters the water to release microscopic larvae. At this stage of the early life of the fiddler crab, the larvae are called *zoeae*.

The larva goes on to live, swim and feed in the open water as plankton. The zoeae undergo a rudimentary process of molting and shedding their outer suits only to develop a new, sturdier exterior. The older fiddler larva is called a *megalopa*. It is during this final stage of the post-larvae fiddler when they molt into juvenile crabs. The

Chapter Three: The Life Cycle of a Fiddler

amount time spent on from the larvae stage to the immature crab stage is different for the species in general.

It typically takes a few weeks to a few months for the crabs to get big enough to find the shoreline. Both the male and female juvenile fiddler crabs look alike at this young stage of their lives. As they grow larger in size, the distinct sexual features of the male from the female become more apparent as the male's claw grows in size. Once the fiddler crabs come into full maturity, the crabs start courting practices, begin to mate again and the cycle continues.

Limb Regeneration

Animal communication is nature's way for animals to accurately get across true information. There are, however, some individuals of particular specie that would give deceptive signals that give wrong information. It is believed that these signals that cheat of the correct information is used to entice mates or ward of competition. It is believed these incorrect signals are used when the particular animal

Chapter Three: The Life Cycle of a Fiddler

wouldn't be able to do if it were to signal truthfully. It has been noted that some species of fiddler crabs signal deceptively.

When a fiddler crab autotomized their large claw, that is when they shed off this large clawed limb, they are able to regenerate the limb through a process of molting and grow a new one. The new claw usually grows on the opposite side of where the crab lost the claw. In most times, fiddlers can regenerate a new claw that is identical to the one it lost. However, in others, the new claw that the fiddler has regenerated can appear very different from the original claw that was lost.

The newly regenerated claw is notably lacking teeth, it is smaller and more delicate than the one it had initially grown into from when it was growing. Although male fiddler crabs are able to regenerate a new claw with generally the same length as the lost one, the smaller claw lacks in power and muscle mass making it a less effective weapon. However, on the other hand, the less heavy, newly generated claw is lighter to lift thereby making it a better

Chapter Three: The Life Cycle of a Fiddler

tool for waving at females. Although it is less effective as a bluff to fight with, it may be that males prefer the lighter version of the new limb because it does seem to attract the ladies more.

When a fiddler crab feels there is a threat to its territory, it uses its massive claw to fight off would be over takers. The male fiddler would square off with strangers who approach their burrow and fight them for ownership. Fiddler crabs also fight amongst themselves and mark their territorial boundaries.

Fiddler crabs are wearier of strangers than their usual neighbors since the presence of strangers ups the chances of them losing their burrow and giving up their territory than if they were merely warding off their neighbor from encroaching on their piece of land. Losing to a stranger usually would be followed by the fiddler giving up ownership of the burrow whereas losing to a neighbor would equate a reduction in its general territory. But it is

Chapter Three: The Life Cycle of a Fiddler

interesting to know that disputes amongst neighbors fiddler crabs are not settled through brute force.

The aggression is used as a sort of punishment to give reminder to the encroaching neighbor to not attempt overtaking the usual territory of the fiddler crab.

Molting

A fiddler crab undergoes a stressful but necessary process of molting throughout its lifetime. It is a stressful process that takes away significant energy from the fiddler. The process basically renders the little fiddler crab, vulnerable to predators because of its "naked" state. Therefore it is important for someone who is considering a fiddler crab to understand this. It is imperative that the fiddler crab, in this state, be given the proper space to expand.

Molting is a crab's way of growing and regenerating limbs they may have lost. Molting is also the manner for fiddler crabs to eliminate harmful toxins which is usually

Chapter Three: The Life Cycle of a Fiddler

concentrated on the chitin, this is the fibrous substance which in part makes up the exoskeleton of the crabs body. You will notice slight coloration changes in your fiddler crabs about two to three days before it starts molting. They take on a lighter brown to purplish shade as the new cuticle pushes out the old exoskeleton. The shed shell is also a way for the crab to get much needed calcium at this time of its vulnerable state.

And because they are much more susceptible to being a predator's dinner during this period, crabs tend to be very cautious, preferring to be left alone and hidden away. Aside from the color changes noticed from the crab, the fiddler also becomes less active and will stop feeding. It has been observed that just a few hours before your crab complete its molt it will be very still.

Do not be alarmed, this is natural. The fiddler is not to be touched or moved during this time, no matter how tempting. Being vulnerable this way, other fiddler crabs may

Chapter Three: The Life Cycle of a Fiddler

take advantage of this and show aggression toward the molting fiddler.

Young fiddler crabs molt more often than the mature ones. Average aged, post-juvenile, fiddler crabs molt around every eight weeks. The crab's outer skin, its exoskeleton, should begin separating from its cuticle right around ten days before the old one is totally shed. The complete removal of the old shell, once ready to fall off, only takes around 15 minutes for some fiddler crabs.

The hardening of the shell, however, takes a tad longer but should complete itself after several days. During this time, the fiddler crab needs more water and calcium, which it usually gets from its newly shed exoskeleton. A fiddler crab seen to feed on its old shell is believed to be taking in the calcium provided by its shed exoskeleton. Once the molting period is accomplished and completed, the fiddler crab goes back to its usual busy lifestyle.

Chapter Four: Common Modern Day Stressors

Knowing what to expect when taking in a new pet to care for is really the wise thing to do. And this is why you are here reading all about the fiddler crab. Getting to know what the potential pet is like, its behavior and characteristics, are important points you will need to pay mind to because the information you get about the pet allows you to give them the best possible care.

Chapter Four: Common Modern Day Stressors

It is important to understand the features of each stage of its life so that you are not caught unawares of anything that may otherwise seem amiss or unusual. For instance, some crabs when molting would be turned upside down with its belly sticking up in the air. If you didn't know this, you might just think they had keeled over. Hold the funeral! Some crabs actually do that. And crabs at the stage of molting should never be touched or moved until nature has completed the process of replacing its old shell for a new one.

Keeping any pet safe and healthy is and should be the primary and main concerns of a potential pet keeper. Taking charge of raising a pet should be kept humane and should only be considered by responsible individuals who are ready to put in the proper research as to how to take care of the pet that will eventually be joining their home life. Pet care is not only an enjoyable hobby but it can also be lucrative in terms of investment and resale if one is so inclined toward the commerce of pet fiddler crabs.

Chapter Four: Common Modern Day Stressors

In this chapter we shall be discussing the behavioral features of the fiddler crab in various times of its life cycle. We shall be discussing the details to watch out for and how to deal with any changes that occurs naturally due to territorial disputes, mating and other important factors about the fiddler crab that is important to keep in mind if you do in fact intend to raise a couple or more for yourself.

Discover the intricate dance of courtship of the massively clawed fiddler crab and find out how they behave in everyday life. Get to know them from a closer perspective in this section.

Courtship Rituals and Mating Process of Fiddler Crabs

Fiddler crabs are diurnal and are active beings during the day. They spend their most of their time foraging for food to feed them. The rest of the time is spent burrowing deep tunnels and getting the attention of the ladies. The burrow is an important aspect of the fiddler crab's day as it is vital to their daily grind since the mouth of the burrow is

Chapter Four: Common Modern Day Stressors

where they would usually find their sustenance. The burrow is where the fiddler crabs secrets away to rest when night falls.

Another reason for the burrow is to prepare for a place where the male fiddler woos and mates with a female fiddler. While many fiddler crabs and lay in wait for a female to wander into the nest so they can mate with it, there are other species of fiddler crabs who have a different method of courtship.

Some of these crabs would make and prepare a burrow and would stand outside of the burrow's mouth waiting for a female to go in first before they follow. Researchers who had been extensively been researching fiddler crabs suppose that this is done because of the stiff competition between males to get the attention of the females. Females who go into the burrow first increase the chances of the male fiddlers mating successfully with the female; the males would stand by the mouth of the tunnel and wave their big claw to attract the attention of the female.

Chapter Four: Common Modern Day Stressors

The premise that if the female enters first, the male is able to trap them with no way out once they have the female in the burrow. The male who coerces the female in would follow the female shortly and plug up the entrance of the tunnel. Males face a complicated courtship with females because of the competition around them. A female may have to choose from up to 20 male fiddlers before they make their choice. The females pick their partners based on multiple factors which include the male's size, the coloration of the claw and the ability to wave the claw during courtship.

Typically, once male gets the attention of the female, the male enters the burrow first and the female, if enticed by what she sees, will follow. However, sometimes, the male courting a female would step aside. The thinking of researches on this strategy of the males is that once the female is inside, the likelihood of a successful mating is higher. It has also been suggested that females who enter the burrow first were likelier to lay eggs than females who entered after the males.

Chapter Four: Common Modern Day Stressors

Breeding Process of Fiddler Crabs

The male fiddler is also able to make a sound thumping on the forest floors, and muddy banks. It uses its massive claw to build burrowed nesting grounds where it attracts female fiddlers. Female fiddler crabs are finicky about the quality of the burrow that the male tunnels. The sturdiness of the burrow signals to the female that this is a good incubation site; therefore it is in their best interest to check out the digs first before actually choosing to mate with the male.

The pulsations and the vibrations the males gives off whilst waving at the female to attract her, gives good indication to the female fiddler about the size and physique of the male fiddler. The longer the male fiddler is able to hold up its huge claw and wave it at the female the likelier that the female will be attracted to them. There are of course other things the female fiddler will have to consider before they choose a male partner. The burrow is one of the more

Chapter Four: Common Modern Day Stressors

important deal closers between the male and female fiddler crabs.

Fiddler crabs develop an uncompromising spatial distance between where they are in proximity to their burrow. Keeping a short distance between themselves and their burrow allows them to scuttle back to their hideout should there be any form of danger. They are able to scamper back when surprised by movement, even without making visual contact with the entrance of the burrow. Nature has gifted the beasts of the animal kingdom the ability to navigate their path by integrating direction and distance based on their movements.

Fiddler crabs use their claws to forage for organic waste in order to feed themselves. While the female crab has two equal sized claws that they both use to shovel food into their mouths, the male only utilizes its smaller claw to feed itself. Since the males are only able to feed themselves with one claw, it takes them more time to forage until they are satiated. The minor claw of the male fiddler is used to filter bits of organic food it collects from the shores of its habitat.

Chapter Four: Common Modern Day Stressors

These crabs collect their sustenance by scraping sediment by use of their small claws. It then transports and transfers the food they collect to the mouth.

A complex course of events happens next when the fiddler crab's mouthparts sort out the organic matter that they feed on. Once they have sorted through what they just put in their mouth, they spit out a small pellet of sand that has been stripped clean of any nutrients and food matter that is essential to the fiddler.

Co - Dependency of Fiddler Crabs

These crabs are intertidal creatures that inhabit sandbars, mudflats, mangrove forests, tidal and tidal creeks. Fiddler crabs are aplenty all over the world and there can be some of them that inhabit stone and boulder coastlines. Fiddler crabs occur in vast numbers and they can be quite a sight to witness.

Thousands upon thousands of them live in close proximity to each other and populate adjacent territories.

Chapter Four: Common Modern Day Stressors

Male and female fiddler crabs live amongst each other and intermingle freely. However, each fiddler crab has its own burrow surrounded by an area of surface sediment. The mention of the importance of the burrow is worth repeating because it is also where the fiddler crab takes refuge during high tide. When the tide ebbs, the water helps keep the gills of the fiddler crab wet. The burrow is also a refuge the fiddler crab can duck into in the presence of danger and predators. And to top it all off, the burrow is also where the mating happens as well as a safe, incubation site for the female.

The male fiddler crab uses its massive claw to entice the less aggressive females into mating with them. It also uses it to repel other males who they consider as competition. When the female fiddler is ready to mate, which is as frequent as once a month, it leaves her burrow in search for the best male candidate to mate with. She would normally follow a male into his burrow and will begin inspection of the quality of the tunnel. If the burrow is substandard to the liking of the female she would then wander out in search of the next burrow to check out. When a female fails to reappear after entering the male's burrow, this signals approval from her that the burrow as with the male is acceptable for a mating place and a mate. If the female does not emerge from the burrow the male will then proceed to plug up the entrance of the burrow and commence mating with the female.

The female fiddler crab times the mating in order for the egg release to coincide with the spring tide. During this period, the egg laden female releases her eggs during the nocturnal tide, when the tiny larva swims into deep waters. There in the deep, the tiny larvae of fiddler crabs develop for several weeks until they are washed up to the shore. This is when the juvenile fiddler crabs undergo the process of a final molt of their young lives, and turn out as tiny, little fiddler crabs.

This is when these young fiddler crabs begin their existence on marsh banks and mudflats. Fiddler crabs are not overly sensitive pets that need a bit of consideration to

Chapter Four: Common Modern Day Stressors

get by. They are not as fragile and finicky as some aquatic species are. However, it is important for the potential keeper to understand what to expect when expecting to raise fiddler crabs as much as they have simplistic needs in terms of habitat. That is another thing we will be discussing later.

Chapter Four: Common Modern Day Stressors

Chapter Five: To Catch or to Buy?

Because of the frequency of occurrence of the fiddler crab, it can be pretty easy to come across a couple or so if you know where to look. They can be found in marshlands, swampy areas, river, and lagoon banks. They can also be spotted in multitude on beaches where they look for food, feed and mate. Fiddler crabs will be found in high numbers

Chapter Five: To Catch or to Buy?

where they can get their claws on organic matter like algae that they can feed on. The internet is one place where you can do your initial "digging". There are countless forums where like - minded fiddler caregivers congregate to talk about their experiences. Joining a forum is also a good place to read about best practices. You can find out about how successful fiddler caretakers set up their aquariums.

The most obvious place is at a pet store where they can be found. There are a couple of considerations to remember, however, should you choose to look for fiddlers at your local pet shop. First off, be mindful that the fiddler crab thrives in semi-salty, brackish water. Some pet shops may be misled to place fiddler crabs in freshwater. You will want to avoid this.

Fiddler crabs may be able to withstand freshwater for a little while but it won't for long. Should this be the case, the fiddler crabs will surely expire soon after. And while it is true that a female fiddler crab will reproduce in captivity, there is no certainty that the eggs will be reared successfully.

Chapter Five: To Catch or to Buy?

Since female fiddler crabs carry their eggs in their belly, it is not at all impossible for them to get impregnated by a male partner. However, the missing factor to the success is the absence of the deep blue. A fiddler crab lays its eggs in the water.

These eggs are then carried out to the ocean and there they float and eventually hatch as swimming larvae or plankton. And it is out in deep ocean where they grow. Once they are mature crabs, they are brought back by the tide, as they swim, to shore. A successful breeding would then be quite impossible to accomplish in an aquarium.

Where to Buy or Find Fiddler Crabs

There are a number of places where one can purchase fiddler crabs. Since fiddler crabs are also used for fishing you may be able to find quite a bit at bait shops. That could be a good place to find, or make arrangements for the purchase of good, healthy candidates who can share space and occupy the aquarium you will be preparing for them.

Chapter Five: To Catch or to Buy?

Do make sure that you will be getting one's that have been placed in brackish water or run the absolute risk of them expiring. If given the proper conditions in the environment that you provide for it, these hardy little guys are easy to care for and an amusing addition to any tank that will be housing friendly sorts that they get on with well. Fiddler crabs are not fully aquatic. They are able to thrive on land and water, but will need an equal amount of time on both land and water to live a pleasant existence.

- A pet supply store is another good place to ask around
- Consider going on fiddler crab care forums online to find out where you can purchase one.
- You can also go online to find out where fiddler crabs are spotted and go on an expedition. We listed a few techniques on how to catch a few of these fellows, below. NOTE: Release the ones that you will not be bringing home with you. Remember that these little guys do us and the Earth a great service of oxygenating the soil much needed by the trees that produce our air.

Chapter Five: To Catch or to Buy?

- You may want to check out nearby marshes, lagoons, riverbanks, or even better, nearby beaches.

Fiddler crabs are aplenty around mangrove and salt marshes. They can also be spotted in muddy and sandy beaches living and foraging on mudflats. Found in the regions of the Western Atlantic and the Eastern Pacific, fiddler crabs can be easily recognized because of their square, chunky carapace and they would certainly stand out because of their one massive claw.

Fiddler crabs are essential to the growth to mangroves and forests because of their burrowing habits. They tunnel through the soil in order to find a place to molt, rest and most especially, mate. The act of fiddler crabs burrowing underneath the soil allows the soil of the marsh, river, streams or lagoon bed to aerate. So be sure that if you are harvesting fiddler crabs from these sites that you only take what you will be able to comfortably take care of, and no more.

Chapter Five: To Catch or to Buy?

How to Catch Fiddler Crabs

If you are catching your fiddler crabs from a beach, look for the area where they are concentrated the most. You might have to do a little investigative work and find out what time they congregate in a particular area before setting out traps.

Once you have determined the area where they frequent most, you can start planning and plotting locations. The beauty of this is that you get to spend a day or two by the beach as you wait for your little buddies to come around. Bring with you a few deep, light colored pails. The light colored pails are the least that would absorb heat from the sun, making sure that your fiddler crab catch is preserved for when they are brought home.

Fishermen who trap fiddler crabs to use as bait bring big deep buckets in order to get the largest possible number of fiddlers. You will only need a couple of small ones since you will be bringing home just a few at the very most.

Chapter Five: To Catch or to Buy?

- Scout for crab holes in the area of your choice. These will be easy to spot if indeed fiddler crabs live and forage here. Active burrows will be easy to spot because of the small mounds that are built near the burrows.
- Dig a hole on the sand, or marsh bank, that is big and deep enough for you to set your bucket in and that is just above the water mark.
- Be careful that you do not damage any of the mangrove roots.
- If you are leaving these buckets out unattended, make sure that there are a few holes on the base of the pail for drainage purposes. You wouldn't want to leave out the bucket without breathing holes. Should it rain, the fiddler crabs will drown before you get back to them. Keep in mind that fiddler crabs breathe surface air.
- Bury the bucket leaving about an inch from the lip above the sand.

Chapter Five: To Catch or to Buy?

- Make a chum mix of fish, and shrimp bits. You may also use commercial chum.
- Mix your chum mixture with the surrounding sand from the area so that birds are kept at bay.
- Fill in the bucket with sand and top it off with the chum mix you had just prepared.
- Sit back, go fish, or sunbathe. You should be able to have a bounty of fiddler crabs in the pail by the end of your downtime.

If you are not really in the digging mood and you don't have the luxury of waiting around for the fiddler crabs to walk into your lair, you may use a cardboard, Styrofoam or plastic box with the bottom hollowed out. In this case, you will have to find the area where the fiddler crabs are most spotted.

The next step is simple; merely toss the box over the area where the fleeing crabs scamper. Be careful picking up your new buddies to bring home. Make sure that you bring them home in an aerated receptacle that has enough water from

Chapter Five: To Catch or to Buy?

where they are from. Make sure that you harvest responsibly! These little guys do the ecology of their habitat a great service by aerating and oxygenating the ground beneath. Be conscientious and mindful.

Chapter Five: To Catch or to Buy?

Chapter Six: Habitat and Maintenance for Fiddler Crabs

Mini crabs can be interesting and very entertaining additions to your collection of terrarium pets. Not only are they great to watch, they can also spruce and liven up a terrarium in new ways that you will soon enjoy. But, if you are bent on getting a couple of these little creatures, you need to make sure that you are aware of how to care for them.

Chapter Six: Habitat and Maintenance for Fiddler Crabs

The fiddler crab can get along well with some water species and would be a joy to watch. The fiddler crab is a crustacean that is fascinating in itself with its active lifestyle.

In this section of the book we shall be looking into how to set up a proper habitat for the fiddler crab. We shall discuss how to set up the best possible ecosystem that will allow them to thrive. A spot specially theirs where they are allowed to be the creatures of intrigue they are.

How to Set Up Your Fiddler Crab Tank

Fiddler crabs are not finicky pets to raise but they do have few specific needs but none so outrageously expensive that it would leave you in a financial fix. You will need a few things that will help create an environment that closely resembles their natural habitat. In order to do this, you will want to purchase a tank that is big enough to hold 10 gallons of water. This size will comfortably house two or three fiddler crabs and will allow them to establish their territories.

Chapter Six: Habitat and Maintenance for Fiddler Crabs

Should you be thinking about getting more than a pair of fiddler crabs, keep in mind that you will need a bigger tank. A small tank with a big population will not be a conducive space. If you plan to get anywhere between four and six, then make sure that you have a tank that is big enough for all of them.

You can get a big tank from a pet store or a retailer. You can also find most of the furnishings and equipment you will need to measure and/or regulate heat, light, mesh, and other sundries for the tank. If you are buying a second hand tank, which you can find online or at flea markets, be sure that you wash and sterilize this thoroughly before you start landscaping and furnishing the tanks' interior. The following are steps you need to remember to set up your fiddler crab tank:

- Since crabs are more active when they are in a warm environment, you want place the tank in a part of a room where it is toasty. Note: Do not place your the tank in direct sunlight or anywhere near where the

Chapter Six: Habitat and Maintenance for Fiddler Crabs

sun rays reach the tank Sunlight can cause mortal harm to the crab.

- Make sure that draft does not get in the room. This can change the room temperature drastically.
- Keep the tank away from the radiator, fireplace or any other heating devices.
- Use a thermometer to measure the temperature in the room and find a spot where the temperature is consistent between 20 to 25 degrees Celsius.

Ensuring that you have the proper room temperature appropriate for the needs of your tank inhabitants, allows for a healthier life and a better life expectancy. You will be able to enjoy a lot of quality moments studying and enjoying your fiddler crabs. Once you are satisfied that the temperature is the proper one, you can set your tank down on that spot. Make sure that it is secure and that the table is sturdy and will not topple. When you have done this you can start working on preparing the inside of the tank.

Chapter Six: Habitat and Maintenance for Fiddler Crabs

You can now add sand to the tank. When adding the sand, take note of the following:

- First consider that crabs are part terrestrial like to burrow. Giving them enough sand to tunnel into will make them really happy campers. They will also need enough depth in order to hide away to when they are undergoing the molting process.

- Second consideration is your idea of how you want to landscape the tank. Once you have fulfilled the first few steps, you may now fashion your tank and mimic the natural habitat of the fiddler crab by providing them slopey beaches that they can crawl up to from the water. Your fiddler crabs will need spaces above the water levels were they can dig, bask and crawl around.

* You can begin with about 5-6 cm of bio, play or aquarium sand adding more as you see fit. Just make sure that the sand does not mound up too high that your

Chapter Six: Habitat and Maintenance for Fiddler Crabs

crabs are able to crawl up and out of the tank. They are clever escape artists.

- Remember to pile more sand on one side of the tank. Your fiddler crab pets will need to get out of the water and will want a place to bask. A sandy slope will somehow mimic their natural environment. You can even fashion two beach slopes if you have a bigger tank.

- When you are happy with the quantity and depth of the sand, you can start filling the tank up with water. Since fiddler crabs inhabit ecosystems that contain natural brackish water, you will need to recreate this.

- Make it a point to use de - chlorinated water because water that isn't de - chlorinated will cause the crabs stress and kill the fiddler crabs.

- Mix a liter and a half to two liters of de - chlorinated water with a half teaspoon or a gram of marine salts.

Chapter Six: Habitat and Maintenance for Fiddler Crabs

- You will notice that the water will turn brownish and cloudy. This will happen, especially more so, when your crawling tenants move in since they will actively be inhabiting the tank doing stuff that fiddler crabs do.

- Alternatively you may also think about putting a wide, shallow dish of water that has been depressed or flushed into the sand. This can be an option for you to consider since you will need to clean out the water often because your fiddler crabs will be eating from there and there will be food remnants that you will want to clear away by throwing out the water and replacing it.

- Make sure that you replace the water frequently to avoid bacteria from festering. When you are happy with the water level, you can start thinking about the furnishings you want to add in.

- Your new fiddler crab tenants need hiding places and nooks where they can hide away when they are molting.

Chapter Six: Habitat and Maintenance for Fiddler Crabs

These can also be good safe havens to duck into when there is any confrontation amongst tenants.

- Since crabs will usually destroy live plants, you can opt to spruce up the tank with plastic plants instead.

- Pepper the sand banks with faux sticks that look like driftwood and rocks. These are great comforting places where they can scamper to and hideaway from their peers when they feel like it.

- A plastic, hollow pipe which is big enough in circumference your fiddler crabs can crawl through is another good addition that will give your new buddies a good exercise.

Be sure that you clean out the pipe and other furnishings well before setting them in the tank. Tank pets that expire are usually attributed to improper tank care and maintenance. When a tank is not clean, especially the water, it becomes a breeding ground for bacteria and virus to fester.

Chapter Six: Habitat and Maintenance for Fiddler Crabs

This affects the health of the residents of the tank and is the leading cause of death in tank pets. You will want to make sure that you sanitize each item before you place them in the tank. You would ideally want to set up the tank with your new crawling tenants on standby for the move. We've already determined that you can order your troop of fiddler crabs online or at a pet supplier in your neighborhood. When they reach you, here are some things to remember before you help them move in to their tank;

- Use a deep bucket or a small tub which you had filled with brackish water (refer back to the solution mix above) to hold your fiddler crabs in.

- Do not allow them to wallow in the water they came with. You must make sure that you dispose of the water they were transported in and immediately transfer them to the buckets with the prepared water solution.

Chapter Six: Habitat and Maintenance for Fiddler Crabs

- You will want to separate the males from the females if they arrived in separate containers.

- You will need to cover these receptacles with a lid, to keep the fiddlers from climbing out and escaping.

Now that you have set up the tank, complete with the proper, needful furnishings, you can now transfer and release the fiddler crabs into the tank. You will want to observe the fiddler crabs closely especially if they are sharing space. Watch out for aggression or tension amongst the mates. Fiddler crabs, by nature, travel together and can get on considering the territorial nature they all share and vie for. These confrontations usually do not result in injury. However, if you notice one lording it over another, limiting the "weaker" one's movement within the tank, you may have to separate them.

Chapter Six: Habitat and Maintenance for Fiddler Crabs

Feeding Your Captive Fiddler Crabs

In their natural habitat, the fiddler crab serves a great purpose in the balance and equilibrium of the territories they inhabit. The act of them foraging for food and feeding is nature's way of enriching the soil, aerating and providing it oxygen. This process of the fiddlers burrowing continuously brings about sediments that are rich in nutrients, up to the surface which they feed on. These sediments later become vital fertilizer which feeds the foliage and plants. The mouthparts of the fiddler crab has developed in a way that they are able to ingest foods which consist of organic animal and plant matter, which they sift out from the sandy, muddy sediments found in marshlands and river banks.

However well you try to recreate the fiddler crabs environment, taking cues from their natural one, there are some things that you will not be able to replicate. For one, unless you are a research lab studying the possibilities of captive reproduction, mating and population growth will

Chapter Six: Habitat and Maintenance for Fiddler Crabs

not be possible. Feeding is another. In captivity, your fiddler pets will need to be fed sinking food.

Some tips for feeding and husbandry of Fiddler Crabs

- They will be able to accept and feed on fish flakes, brine shrimp, and plankton, which you can purchase from your local pet store.

- Bait stores seem like the obvious place to shop. But be careful about how the food is harvested, and how it is stored.

- Feeding might be something you may want to bring up at a forum of fiddler crab keepers. You can, at the very least, read about success stories of other fiddler crab owner/posters.

- You will want to give your fiddler crabs some sort of variety. Switch up the menu with freeze dried bloodworms, and seaweed

Chapter Six: Habitat and Maintenance for Fiddler Crabs

- If you do serve up seaweed, pay mind that this may promote algae growth in the tank, which your fiddler crabs will feast on. Remember that fiddler crabs eat rotting food.

- Do not switch up its diet to human table food because your fiddler crabs will be eating from the water, its quality will deteriorate to a murky mess soon enough. When you begin to notice the smell of ammonia, take this cue and replace the sand and water inside the tank. This will also be a good time to give the tank a good once over.

- Always remember to replace the water in the tank with a brackish solution, using de - chlorinated water regularly

- The water level in the tank will decrease due to evaporation. Pay mind that you replace this with a proper amount of clean, brackish water

Chapter Six: Habitat and Maintenance for Fiddler Crabs

- Should you notice minimal activity from the crabs, it may be as simple as changing the water. Changing the water regularly will promote more active fiddler crabs. Make sure that you replace the water in the tank frequently. Fiddler crabs are a hardy species so illness and disease is rare in them.

- They and all captive aquatic animals for that matter, usually contract illness and disease from the bacteria build up.

- Improper temperatures can also be a cause for illness

Chapter Seven: Common Sub – Species of Fiddler Crabs

With over a hundred species and subspecies of fiddler crabs, it can be a little too much to figure out for ourselves which one is the best sort to take home, study, and raise under our care. Fiddler crabs are easy to spot with their square bodies with a marked difference of claw size amongst male fiddlers. This becomes more apparent as the male fiddler matures.

Chapter Seven: Common Sub – Species of Fiddler Crabs

As it grows, so does the large claw (the cheliped) of the male. From a claw that once took up 2 percent of its body weight, the mature male cheliped makes up 65 percent of the male fiddler's total body weight. Female fiddler crabs share similar shape and coloration with that of the males in their community but can be distinguished because of their smaller and symmetrical claws.

Most male fiddler crabs will likely have an enlarged claw on one side of their carapace. Some may have a left massive claw, whilst others have a massive claw on the right. Fights amongst male fiddler crabs are unavoidable and inevitable. They vie for space and territory; they chase after the same females and survive by foraging the most successfully for sustenance.

Fights between males of the opposite sided big claws are a far cry from males who battle it out with same handed males. When face to face with opposite handedness, their claws go in the same direction. While males with similar sided massive claws have their claws lined up and trained in

Chapter Seven: Common Sub – Species of Fiddler Crabs

the opposite direction of each other. Fiddler crabs that are different handed are able to take stock of the other ones' size. However, those whose claws trained on opposite directions will be able to interlock claws easier. Let's take a more in-depth look at the three most commonly found fiddler crab species in the United States and find out how they are distinct from one another.

Sub – Species of Fiddler Crabs

Mud Fiddler Crab (*Uca Pugnax*)

The *Uca Pugnax* or the Mud Fiddler Crab is commonly found in the muddy environment of marshlands. They prefer where the substrate is not heavily laden with large plant roots since they need the space underneath and burrow down to about 23 inches deep into the earth. Mud fiddler crabs like the substrate to be stable enough for a construction of this magnitude.

Chapter Seven: Common Sub – Species of Fiddler Crabs

Mud fiddler like to lift their massive claw in the air and wave it up and down in the hopes of attracting a female fiddler's attention. This is part of the courtship phase. When males lift up and wave their hand at another male, it is basically to ward off or intimidate their male competition.

Physical and Behavioral Traits:

- Mud fiddlers stomp their legs (their minor, non-clawed appendages)
- They make noises with their walking legs to attract mates
- Mating rituals, displays and pulsations typically reach peak over the spring tides.
- The actual mating happens inside of the confines of the male fiddler's burrow.
- This is where the female incubates her eggs over a two-week period after which she appears above ground to release her eggs in the open sea where it swept out.
- The eggs are swept out by weak tides that happen during nights of the quarter moon.

Chapter Seven: Common Sub – Species of Fiddler Crabs

- The larvae goes through a series of developmental processes once they are hatched
- Larvae prey on zooplankton from the water column
- Over this two week period, the larva is set adrift in the sea and is deposited back to the coastlines during the next spring tide.
- They remain out at sea until such time that they grow out limbs and their appendages are complete.
- The mud fiddler is tinged blue on the top of its carapace as well as its eyestalks
- Male mud fiddlers have a somewhat developed ridge found on their massive claw.
- These little guys are usually spotted in brackish water marshes and muddy river banks
- Mud fiddler crabs can also be found in drier ground in higher intertidal zones where there are patches of grass and hay.
- The mouthparts of the mud fiddler, also known as the marsh crab, has developed and evolved to scrape dead organic matter from the sediments in the mud and sand.

Chapter Seven: Common Sub – Species of Fiddler Crabs

- This specie of fiddler crab is also seen to live and forage amongst the red-jointed fiddler.
- It is also seen to socialize and travel with sand fiddler crabs.
- Mud, or marsh, fiddler crabs grow to about an inch in size (diameter of the carapace across).

Sand Fiddler Crabs (*Uca pugilator*)

Sand fiddlers (Uca pugilator) can be found by the multitude in muddy and brackish intertidal regions. They can be found near salt marshes and spotted in abundance in the banks of tidal creeks where they forage for food. The sand fiddler can also be spotted on surfaces of the marsh most especially when the substrate is composed more of sand than mud. It is not unusual to see an intermingling of sand and mud fiddlers. Here along the marsh tidal creeks of the southeast they congregate to forage for food and feed together.

Chapter Seven: Common Sub – Species of Fiddler Crabs

Physical and Behavioral Traits:

- The sand fiddler's burrow is dug at an angle and has no turn.
- They utilize specialized spoon-like bristles to harvest algae and organic matter.
- They collect algae from sandy deposits which they ball up and deposit into their burrows.
- Sand fiddler crabs can be seen to move and forage with mud fiddlers
- Sand fiddler crabs and red-jointed fiddler crabs are rarely seen to mingle with each other
- The sand fiddler's carapace is a light brown which occasionally has a purple colored blotch.
- The male sand fiddler's massive claw lacks a ridge
- The sand fiddler crabs prefer to congregate and live by the sandy and brackish waters.
- Their mouthparts have evolved and developed to be able to find food in coarse sand to gather and forage for sustenance.
- The maximum size of a sand fiddler is about 1 inch.

Chapter Seven: Common Sub – Species of Fiddler Crabs

Red-jointed Fiddler Crabs (*Uca Minax*)

Red-jointed Fiddler Crabs (Uca Minax) are often found in freshwater tidal marshes that are low in salinity on sandy and muddy substrates that is rich in organic matter important to the nourishment, sustenance and survival of the red-jointed fiddler crab. Red-jointed fiddler crabs like their southeastern cousins, the sand fiddler, ball up sediments of sand rich with organic matter which they feed on.

Physical and Behavioral Traits:
- Red-jointed fiddlers have a tendency to move inland putting space between them and the intertidal zone and the marshes
- The red-jointed fiddler is able to tolerate the lack of oxygen.
- They share the similar feeding habits of the fiddler crabs which populate the southeastern region of the US.

Chapter Seven: Common Sub – Species of Fiddler Crabs

- Aside from the feeding they habits they share with their southeastern cousins, they also share the same biology.
- Red jointed fiddlers can often be seen mingling with mud fiddler crabs, feeding and moving together.
- Red jointed fiddlers are not usually spotted to socialize with mud fiddler crabs.
- The red jointed fiddler crab possesses a yellowish-brown carapace
- Its name hints on this fiddler crabs appearance. The red jointed fiddler has reddish joints between the limbs.
- The red jointed fiddler crab is typically found in areas near bodies of water like brackish marshes.
- It is also found in freshwater marshes and stream banks.
- The red jointed fiddler crab rather likes the lower intertidal zones that are abundant with cord grass.
- This is the only fiddler crab specie that has been noted to be able to survive its entire adult life in freshwater.

Chapter Seven: Common Sub – Species of Fiddler Crabs

- It feeds on dead organic plant and animal matter, but is also likes to prey on larger food bits.
- The red jointed fiddler grows to a maximum size of about 1.5 inches.

Chapter Eight: Distribution and Ecology Status

This chapter will cover the distribution and range of fiddler crabs in general as well as their ecology status. We'll also take a closer look at the specific features of some of the more commonly found fiddler crabs. With close to a hundred sorts and sub-sorts, you will want to be able to learn a little more about the tiny guys who will be sharing space with you. As much as fiddler crabs possess all similarities, each species has a different coloration.

Chapter Eight: Distribution and Ecology Statusc

Distribution

Fiddler crabs can be found in many regions of the world in different countries. They are frequently to be found in salt marshes, on muddy and sandy beaches of the Eastern Pacific, the Western Atlantic, West Africa and the Indo-Pacific regions of the globe. In the United States red-jointed fiddler crabs have a large occurrence along the east and Gulf coasts, from Cape Cod to Texas.

Sand fiddlers can be found along coastlines of Massachusetts all the way down to the western region of Florida. Mud fiddlers are common in marshes along the southeastern coast of the United States. North Carolina seems to be the most conducive to all three Uca specie since they are found throughout the coast of the state and are in extreme abundance. Fiddler crabs are one of the most common inhabitants of intertidal regions of the coast and of the marsh lands where they occur.

Chapter Eight: Distribution and Ecology Statusc

Environmental Status

Fiddler crabs in most Western societies have no commercial value. This cannot be said for other countries where small true crabs, like the fiddler are sold in market and fish ports with a price value that depends on harvest and rarity of catch. Either way, fiddler crabs take on an important role in the balance in the ecology of salt marshes. Fiddler crabs make excellent indicators of environmental imbalance because of their sensitivity to contaminants in the environment, such as pesticides, fertilizers and other biochemical waste.

Their occurrences in high numbers speak of the high productivity of the marshes they occupy. Their burrowing activity affects the soil and sediment of the land they inhabit, allowing for oxygen to move and flow, giving way to a healthy ecosystem. The stimulation that happens when fiddler crabs are actively doing what they do, gives way to the turnover and mineralization of the soil.

Chapter Eight: Distribution and Ecology Statusc

And because they feast on decayed plantation, they hold important roles in the decomposition of plant matter. They, in turn, are prey to animals that thrive in estuarine conditions inclusive of but not limited to blue crabs and all sorts of marsh birds.

The Uca Pugnax or the Mud Fiddler Crab has an H-shaped depressed by nature onto the center of its carapace. They have long, thin eyestalks. They are predominantly brown in color except for the top of the carapace and the tips of the eyes, which range from blue to turquoise. Typical of the large claw of the mud fiddler is a coloration of yellowish orange to a combination of yellowish white. The inside region of the claws of a mud fiddler is lined with a slanted row of tubercles, the round and raised protrusions in the inner part of the claw extends from tip to the wrist cavity of the crab, The walking legs of the mud fiddler is banded and dark.

The Uca pugilator or the Sand Fiddler Crab usually has a pinkish-purple coloration. At the center of the sand fiddler's back are an even brighter hue of purple, and the

Chapter Eight: Distribution and Ecology Statusc

color of their legs range from orange to brown. A marked distinction of the tubercles of the sand fiddler is that it is missing a row compared to that of the other Uca species.

The Uca Minax is also known in the trade as the Red-jointed Fiddler Crab and they are notably larger in size than those of the two previously described species. Another distinguishing factor is the row of red tubercles that line the inner palm of the claw. The red-jointed fiddler also lacks density on the soft down hairs on its second walking leg's ventral margin.

Chapter Eight: Distribution and Ecology Statusc

Chapter Nine: Challenges of the Species

It is pretty amazing how extensively universities and researchers study the fiddler crab. As many species that had been discovered, each one of these crab species under the Uca genus has been studied, documented and recorded extensively. Researchers are interested about their behavior, their asymmetric claws, the way they use their massive claw in for signaling and attracting their mates. Fiddler crabs have been studied in relation to gender selection and their evolutionary development.

Chapter Nine: Challenges of the Species

Their diversity compels researchers in the attempt to define them for their particular features and distinctions from each other. Because of the diversity of the genus with the many varying distinctions of species and subspecies, there has been an open debate about classification of some subspecies.

The fiddler crab has one of the more extreme forms of physical asymmetry amongst any other bilateral creature. And this is attributed to the male's massively huge claw that looks out of place. The claw of the male fiddler crab does not serve the male fiddler crab unless it is to catch the attention of a female or to ward off a potential male competition.

Every other species and subspecies of fiddler crabs was seen to have slight variation in claw waving. All of the primary species of fiddler crabs possess different colors of carapace, aside from the distinctive variation of hues that identify them. They are terrific barometers that give clue to the health and wellness of the ecological system they inhabit.

Chapter Nine: Challenges of the Species

This is because fiddler crabs are very sensitive to a lot of contaminant manufactured by humans. Chemicals that are used as fertilizer will have a great depressive effect on the health of the population of fiddler crabs because these tiny crabs concentrate the toxins they ingest from food or seawater.

The fiddler stores up these toxic chemicals such as PCBs (polychlorinated biphenyls) from contaminated sediments. This in turn is transferred to the terrestrial, avian and aquatic networks. Since these little guys are preyed upon by animals such as fish in the ocean, birds in the air and mammals from the land, these secreted toxins are passed on through the hierarchy of the food chain. Once contaminated fiddler crabs are eaten by a predator, the cycle of the toxin being passed on is in motion.

How these fertilizer toxins affect the fiddler crabs is that the chemicals impaired movement, and killing a chunk of the population of fiddler crabs in a rapid rate. It is due to the chemical contaminants present in some marsh waters that

Chapter Nine: Challenges of the Species

kill these crabs in high concentration. The chemical that seep into the sediment, from which the fiddler crabs, gets its sustenance stays in their system long after it has been ingested by the crabs. Fiddler crabs have also been noted to have very low tolerance for mercury.

The populations of crabs in some areas have been noted to be sensitive to cadmium, too. Wherever lost populations of fiddler crabs are noted, it has been investigated and attributed to the high levels of one sort of chemical or another. These fertilizer and insecticide chemicals radically change up the soil quality, in effect, poisoning it. This in turn affects the wildlife of any particularly contaminated body of water or region of land.

It has been observed that fiddler crab larvae which showed stunted development and growth as well as limb deformities displayed the presence of heavy metals like, copper, zinc and mercury in their systems. Studies have shown that spraying mosquito insecticide in marsh habitats

Chapter Nine: Challenges of the Species

to control the incidence of the pesky biting - buzzers also lowers the occurrence of fiddler crabs in the marsh region.

Other factors that cause a negative impact on the ecosystems of marshy areas and decrease the quality of water in affected regions are roads and golf courses. Golf courses not only encroach on what would've once been areas of animal habitats and waterways. They also use a lot of fertilizers to maintain a lush green field of grass. The runoff water from these as well as residential areas and neighborhoods have an impact on the water quality which in turn affects the marsh creek ecosystems of regions that have been affected.

A small amount can easily dilute in creeks and streams. The situation becomes alarming when the combination of all these chemicals along with other toxic matter is deposited in significant amounts all at once. Contaminants that pollute the lands, toxic chemicals that originate from residential areas, from roads, from commercial establishments and golf greens disrupt the food

Chapter Nine: Challenges of the Species

web in salt marsh. These toxic substances kill off species as it promotes the increase in number of others.

Some fiddler crab populations in some parts of the globe, like the East Coast of India, are threatened due to the occurrence of people and industrialization. Due to the growth of commerce and industry, abundance in some fiddler crab species is on a moderate decline. Three such species are the Uca lactea, Uca annulipes, and the Uca rosea. Not only has human interference been seen as one reason for the decline of these fiddler species, but the high occurrence of waste and pollution is to be blamed as well. These fiddler crabs are vital in indicators of changes in the ecology of an ecosystem of the regions they inhabit. These three fiddler crab species will be vital to the identification of errors and the survival of the species.

Chapter Nine: Challenges of the Species

Accomplishments in Conservation

South-carolina, where the 3 primary species of fiddler crabs are found in the United States has recognized the difficulties in controlling nonpoint-source pollutants. Nonpoint-source pollutants can come from rainfall or snowmelt. A remedy has been adopted in a lot of South Carolina communities to buffer the impacts of these instances of contamination. When water quality in the wetlands are maintained at the proper balance and restored, fiddler crabs are able to thrive better and healthier.

This is a good time to remember that if you are planning on catching local fiddler crabs from wetlands, marsh or beach areas in your locality, it is advisable only to take what you are able to care for and release the rest. With the service that fiddler crabs give to us, by way of turning marsh, and river banks substrate. In order to evaluate recovery impacts of the habitat, fiddler burrow density is studied.

Chapter Nine: Challenges of the Species

Chapter Ten: Summary and Care Sheet

So far we have learnt that there are a number of species of fiddler crabs that populate coastal regions of the United States. All the way from Massachusetts to Florida and Texas to Florida, the hardworking and active fiddler crabs populate these regions by the multitude and do the ecosystems the live in a huge favor. They toil in the soil and substrate of these marsh creeks, allowing for better oxygenation of the lands. Fiddler crabs are found in brackish water, stream banks and lower intertidal zones.

Chapter Ten: Summary and Care Sheet

The fiddler crab has been a well - researched specie of the Uca family because of the many varieties of color, and characteristics each individual species and subspecies possess. Observing fiddler crabs can be entertaining, enjoyable as it is educational, since its mating and territorial orchestrations in its natural habitat can be witnessed easily by a casual observer using a pair of binoculars.

All you would need to do is to sit quietly for a few minutes and the fiddler crabs will surely start its usual activities. They begin to do a number of compellingly fascinating movements. Fiddler crabs move around in droves and can be usually seen in multitude.

All the three most commonly found species in the United States, the Mud Fiddler Crab, the Sand Fiddler Crab and the Red-jointed Fiddler Crab burrow underground to make suitable mating locations for the females they attract into their burrow. These three fiddler crab species all produce stipulations that are considered to be a mating call that male

Chapter Ten: Summary and Care Sheet

fiddlers make. They repeatedly move and tap their legs as they wave their massive claw in the air.

The frequency of these vibrations and pulsations give indication to the female fiddlers of the size and stamina of the male fiddler. These little crabs like to be surrounded in environments where there is brackish water where they scavenge for food particles which they collect in the sand. With their claws the food particles are balled up into little pellets which the promptly deposit into their mouth.

Once they have collected the organic particles from these tiny balled up sand, they dispense of the sand in tiny pellets that typically flank the mouths of the burrow they created. These hardworking crabs that show a lot of attitude and charisma have an important role in keeping the balance of the marsh in which they occur.

Through their feeding activities they regulate production and decomposition of the fauna of the ecosystem of the region they can be found. They are important to the diet of

Chapter Ten: Summary and Care Sheet

bigger animals of the region they inhabit due to their size and place in the food chain. They are preyed upon by herons, egrets, other crabs, raccoons and rails. The sand crab can also prey upon other fiddler crabs occasionally. They gather in large clusters on mud flats and sandy beaches to feed on microorganisms and disintegrated matter from animals and plants.

They travel, feed and socialize in large clusters for the same reasons that other animal species congregate. The large numbers provide a sort of protection from predators of the area.

Male fiddler crabs are combative of the territory they wish to possess. They vie with other male fiddler crabs for space and the attention of female mates. They combat using force, pushing and shoving other male fiddlers of the drove. Male fiddlers would grip and fling each other. They club each other with their huge claw and employ their claws as if they were clubs, flinging and hitting their opponent. They stand their ground, or scamper and flee only to position

Chapter Ten: Summary and Care Sheet

themselves to lunge at their opponent. They make threatening sounds by tapping the earth or the ground beneath them. They stamp their legs, or rub them together that produce sounds to ward off their aggressor.

Each species of fiddler crab has a distinct manner of waving their huge claw at female fiddler crabs. This has been observed by many researchers who have had access to watching these fascinating creatures.

Fiddler crabs that inhabit sandy shores of coast lines of the southeastern border of the United States, once ready to spawn their eggs, travel out of their burrow, from a two week incubation period in the burrow, to release their eggs, which can number up to the thousands, into the open sea. Here in the deep, the fiddler larvae, or the zoeae, float and feed off zooplankton from water columns until such time that the tide brings them back onto shore.

At this time, the fiddler crabs would have grown all their limbs and appendages. It is also during this time when the

Chapter Ten: Summary and Care Sheet

females are easier to spot by way of the male fiddler crab's claw growth rate.

Fiddler crabs, in the event of losing a limb, are able to regenerate complete limbs. Male fiddler crabs are able to regrow a lost massive claw and this may occur on the opposite side of where the former massive claw was. These little crustaceans molt on a regular basis. When they do, remember to leave them alone. Do not attempt to move or touch them. You may want to start keeping a journal keeping notations of the milestones, changes and behaviors of your fiddler crabs. You may also note down the food you feed your crabs, the amount and the frequency of feeding. Fiddler crabs are active and hardworking crabs in their natural habitat.

When they are not trying to woo a female fiddler, they spend the rest of their time foraging for food and feeding themselves. This should give you an indication of how often you should feed them. Ideally, these tiny crabs a favorite subject to study not only by researchers but are often a

Chapter Ten: Summary and Care Sheet

favorite pet in school classrooms are eager eaters, so expect to feed them daily. Aside from frozen worms, hermit crabs can also make a good substitute to serve up to your crabs. You will have to make sure to not leave uneaten food in their tank. Clear these out to avoid infestation of bacteria.

Fiddler crabs are territorial but that doesn't mean they can't share space. As long as you make sure that each crab has enough space, they will have no problem skirting each other some days, and crossing paths on others. Should you fancy adding other species to keep your fiddler crabs company, you may consider other semi-aquatic animals that they can get along with like newts, African frogs, zebra snails, and anoles. You may opt to decorate your semi-aquatic pets tank with real plants, but you will have to be ready to replace them soon after as the crabs will destroy it.

The lifespan of a fiddler crab in captivity is two years, but there have been numerous reports of fiddler crabs in captivity who surpass the two year mark. Your fiddler crabs

Chapter Ten: Summary and Care Sheet

will not be able to repopulate in a tank because the deep sea is a vital component in the growth of the fiddler crab.

Tips in Taking Care of Fiddler Crabs

- Make sure that the tank you purchase for your fiddler crabs is big enough for the number of crabs it will be housing.
- Make certain that the tank is clean and sanitized.
- Be sure to use the recommended sand in the tank, with one side higher, creating a sandy beach from which the crabs can crawl on to and out of the water.
- Do not use chlorinated water in the tank. This will stress out and eventually kill the fiddler crabs.
- Put one or two smooth rocks that can double as refuge for your fiddler crabs. Do not saturate the tank with rocks as fiddler crabs can get equally stressed trying to scamper on rocks.
- Make certain that the tank is positioned in a warm part of the room. If you need to regulate the

Chapter Ten: Summary and Care Sheet

temperature in the room, you may adjust your thermostat to the proper and conducive temperature.

- Be sure to watch for aggression or constant intimidation by one fiddler crab to another. They may have to be separated.
- Make sure to replenish water that has evaporated in the tank using the proper mixture to create a brackish habitat
- Your fiddler crab pet may lose a limb somewhere along the way. Do not panic. If you give it the proper environment, where it can skitter away to, it will regrow its limb.

The Crab in Pop Culture

All creatures great and teeny are pretty fascinating beings. What with the individuality and uniqueness of each of these beings. The crab is a pretty amazingly unique animal that even myth and astrology has paid homage to it by way of identifying it with an astrological sign. A crab

Chapter Ten: Summary and Care Sheet

often depicts the constellation of Cancer in Western astrology.

Cancer is one of the cardinal signs of water. The ruling planet of Cancer is the Moon, and this sign is considered a negative sign. No, there isn't any value judgment associated with negativity. It is perhaps the polarity of the magnet it is likened to; one side being positive, the other negative, neither good nor bad, just different. Those born between the days of June 22 to July 22 are considered Cancerians, depending on the astrology they subscribe to. It is a northern sign, which in the ancient times was thought of as a dark sign because the constellation is located in a place that is visibly obscured in the night sky.

Cancerians are said to have phlegmatic personalities, who would look into themselves rather than talking to people about things that bother and concern them. They are not easily excited by anything and are pretty relaxed people. They are said to be night movers, more comfortable with activity during the night.

Chapter Ten: Summary and Care Sheet

Cancerians are tenacious individuals who will stop at nothing once their hearts are set on something. It is said that Cancerians are lazy and indolent. People born during this period of the year are said to be intuitive as they are emotional. They are said to be refined. Cancerians are thought to be clairvoyant.

Cancer is considered to be the most sensitive sign according to many astrologers. They have the inclination to look at the world and judge things around them through intuition instead of logic. They can be highly spiritual individuals. They are characterized by ambition. They are characterized as enigmatic individuals.

So, you see, crabs are not only prevalent in the physical world we live in; they are also represented in the science of astrology and are some notable characters in fables, legends and myths.

Chapter Ten: Summary and Care Sheet

We hope that you will be able to enjoy your own little fiddler crab habitat. To this day, researchers are drawn to this enigmatic creature which continues to capture the imagination and stir intrigue with their great diverse sorts. Being able to observe them up close on a regular basis will not give you an opportunity to become entertained by these little creatures; they are a joy to observe in terms of their behavior and characteristics. We hope you enjoy many years of watching pleasure as you raise a small troop of fiddler crabs at home.

Photo Credits

Page 10 Photo by user Sheilovealways via Pixabay.com, https://pixabay.com/en/she-crab-fiddler-crab-brackish-1245373/

Page 19 Photo by user Kohei Tanaka via Pixabay.com, https://pixabay.com/en/ariake-sea-fiddler-crab-saga-2787401/

Page 29 Photo by user Jennie Coyote via Pixabay.com, https://pixabay.com/en/fiddler-crab-crab-beach-269470/

Page 40 Photo by user Ozzy Mosis via Pixabay.com, https://pixabay.com/en/crab-taiwan-animal-nature-beach-703395/

Page 52 Photo by user Photo Jeff via Flickr.com, https://www.flickr.com/photos/61123283@N00/2601331830/

Page 61 Photo by user Sek Keung Lo via Flickr.com, https://www.flickr.com/photos/losk/3686603811/

Page 76 Photo by user Andrew Cannizzaro via Flickr.com, https://www.flickr.com/photos/acryptozoo/36118051311/

Page 87 Photo by user Andrea Westmoreland via Flickr.com, https://www.flickr.com/photos/andrea_pauline/4455834714/

Page 93 Photo by user Wilfredorrh via Flickr.com,
https://www.flickr.com/photos/wilfredor/16451253576/

Page 101 Photo by user Tracie Hall via Flickr.com,
https://www.flickr.com/photos/twobears2/32804858952/

References

Evolutionary variation in the mechanics of fiddler crab claws – NIH.gov
https://www.ncbi.nlm.nih.gov/pmc/articles/PMC3716949/

Fiddler Crabs – The Spruce
https://www.thespruce.com/fiddler-crabs-1237222

Fiddler Crabs – URI.edu
http://www.edc.uri.edu/restoration/html/gallery/invert/fiddler.htm

Fiddler Crabs – 2nchance.info
http://www.2ndchance.info/fiddler.htm

Fiddler Crabs – SC. gov
http://www.dnr.sc.gov/cwcs/pdf/FiddlerCrab.pdf

Fiddler Crabs – ANU.edu
http://www.biology-assets.anu.edu.au

Fiddler Crabs of the World – NHM.org
https://decapoda.nhm.org/pdfs/15051/15051-001.pdf

Fiddling Around with Fiddler Crabs – VIMs.edu

http://www.vims.edu/~jeff/biology/fiddler.pdf

Fossil and Modern Fiddler Crabs (Uca Tangeri: Ocypodidae) and Their Burrows from SW Spain: Ichnologic and Biogeographic Implications – OUP.com
https://academic.oup.com/jcb/article/33/4/537/2548131

How to Care For Fiddler Crabs – Mom.me
http://animals.mom.me/how-to-care-for-fiddler-crabs-8545106.html

How to Care For Fiddler Crabs – WikiHow.com
https://www.wikihow.com/Take-Care-of-Fiddler-Crabs

Signs of a Molting Fiddler Crab – Mom.me
http://animals.mom.me/signs-molting-fiddler-crab-9115.html

www.ingramcontent.com/pod-product-compliance
Lightning Source LLC
Chambersburg PA
CBHW060844050426
42453CB00008B/813